We might find some squares,
Where they keep the baboons.
There might be some more,
Where they cage the raccoons.

We'll visit the tortoise,
Who lives in his shell.
We might find a circle.
You never can tell.

Let's check out the monkeys,
And chimpanzees, too.
There must be more circles,
Inside of this zoo.

We'll search for rectangles,
Along the hillside.
There are so many places,
Rectangles can hide.

We'll look for rectangles,
Among all the birds.
We'll look down the hill,
At the buffalo herd.

Elephants are big and
Giraffes are so tall.
Do you think we will spot,
Any diamonds at all?

We'll look at the ducks,
And the pelicans, too.
We must find more diamonds,
Inside of this zoo.

We'll look on the hill,
Where the antelope stray.
Do you think we will find,
A triangle today?

We'll look for triangles,
Near bushes and rocks.
We'll search through the cages,
Of eagles and hawks.

See all the flamingos,
Some near and some far.
Let's search high and low,
For the shape of a star.

We might find some stars,
Where the kangaroos play.
We should find a few,
By the end of the day.

Pandas are cute and
Sea lions are smart.
Let's keep up our search,
For the shape of a heart.

We're glad we have found,
Many shapes at the zoo.
We enjoyed our whole day and,
We hope you did, too!